Getting God Involved
How To Activate & Unleash Your Untapped Potential

Leon McDonald, III

Copyright © 2017 by Leon McDonald, III.
All rights reserved. No part of this publication may be reproduced, distributed, or transmitted in any form or by any means, including photocopying, recording, or other electronic or mechanical methods, without the prior written permission of the publisher, except in the case of brief quotations embodied in critical reviews and certain other noncommercial uses permitted by copyright law.

Scripture quotations marked HCSB are taken from the Holman Christian Standard Bible®, Used by Permission HCSB ©1999,2000,2002,2003,2009 Holman Bible Publishers. Holman Christian Standard Bible®, Holman CSB®, and HCSB® are federally registered trademarks of Holman Bible Publishers.

Scripture quotations noted CEV are taken from the Contemporary English Version Copyright © 1991, 1992, 1995 by American Bible Society, Used by Permission.

Scripture quotations noted NKJV are taken from the New King James Version. Copyright © 1982 by Thomas Nelson, Inc. Used by permission. All rights reserved.

Scripture quotations noted MSG are taken from The Message. Copyright © by Eugene H. Peterson 1993, 1994, 1995, 1996, 2000, 2001, 2002. Used by permission of Tyndale House Publishers, Inc.

Scripture quotations noted (NIV) are taken from the New International Version®, NIV®. Copyright © 1973, 1978, 1984, 2011 by Biblica, Inc.™ Used by permission of Zondervan. All rights reserved worldwide. www.zondervan.com The "NIV" and "New International Version" are trademarks registered in the United States Patent and Trademark Office by Biblica, Inc.™

LM3, Inc.
258 S. Gratiot
Mt. Clemens, MI 48043
www.TheWinnersCircleChurch.org

ISBN 13: 978-1-9842-9078-6
ISBN 10: 1-984290-78-9

Printed in the United States of America

DEDICATION

God, as I sit and pen these words, I am in complete awe of who you are and what you have done. You always ask for the first of everything. By principle, it demonstrates that you are priority over everything else. Therefore, I give back to you the gift you gave to me. This book is 100% dedicated to you. Thank you for giving me life when I could have been aborted. Thank you for choosing me when I didn't deserve it. Thank you for using me when I felt unqualified. Thank you for covering me while I was careless. Thank you for being faithful when you could have forsaken me. Thank you for loving me, flaws and all.

God, your mercy has been endless, mistake after mistake. Your grace has been sufficient, case after case. Your love has relentlessly pursued me and reminded me that, even in my brokenness, I have value. Thank you for showing me that no sin, shame, past or pain can separate me from your love. I am overwhelmed by you, grateful to you, and I only desire to please you. Daddy, with a love as strong and pure as yours, to say, "I love you back" seems like it's not enough. I will never be able to pay you back for all you have done. But I take this opportunity, with everything I have in me, to say, "I love you. I pray you are proud. This first work belongs to you!"

CONTENTS

INTRODUCTION 9
1. GET UP 12
2. APPROACH GOD BOLDLY 17
3. AGREE WITH GOD 23
4. GET ORGANIZED 29
5. GET PLUGGED IN 34
6. BREAK THE CYCLE 39
7. FIX YOUR FOCUS 44
8. MAKE ADJUSTMENTS 50
9. PURSUE THE PROMISE 57
10. SHOW CONFIDENCE 63
11. BE THE STAGE 70
12. BE THE CHANGE 75
13. BE CONSISTENT 80
14. STAY IN NEED 85
15. RESISTS THE NOTIFICATION 92
16. FORGET THE PAST 98
17. DEVELP NEW HABITS 103
18. TURN ON THE LIGHT 109
19. EXPRESS YOUR GRATITUDE 115
20. OPERATE IN OBEDIENCE 120
21. BE PATIENT 127
CONCLUSION 132

Getting God Involved

How To Activate & Unleash
Your Untapped Potential

Leon McDonald, III

INTRODUCTION

Getting God Involved began as a theme for our church's New Year's consecration. Never before in the six-year existence of The Winners Circle Church had we started the year by praying and fasting as a corporate body of believers. Of course, we prayed and fasted at other times during the year, but this year was different.

As we prepared to enter 2017, Holy Spirit led us to do something we had never done before to get the results we never dreamed possible. He instructed us to pray for the first 21 days of the year. On each day, we were to meet by conference call at 6 a.m. and 9 p.m. God's promise to us was simple: If we would charge heaven for 21 days, He would release a blessing to cover us the next 12 months. So with faith and expectation, we obeyed and began the journey.

Initially, I simply prepared each day with a word to encourage God's people at our scheduled prayer stops. I thought I was simply giving a motivational, inspirational thoughts to the partners of our church to get their day started with Jesus. But as the days went on, I realized I had stumbled into a kairos moment. Something divine had taken place and I was right in the middle of it. God was using this time of consecration to birth something that would be a blessing to His people and a weapon in the hands of kingdom-minded believers. What started as a prayer call and corporate fast turned into this book. God had you in mind the entire time. While we were praying, God was engineering this moment to help you attack destiny.

HDTV has a wonderful show called *Fixer Upper*. On this show, people possess or purchase homes that have great potential, yet are in need of a facelift. Many times, the homes look beautiful on the outside, yet need major renovation on the inside. It is at this point that they call the experts to assist them in creating a master plan to take their home to the next level. Well my friend, that's where I come in.

Life is much like a house. And many of you may feel like a fixer upper! When things are broken, dysfunctional and not working properly, you reach for tools to repair the problem. Interestingly enough, no one tool alone can fix every issue in a house. Each tool has a unique purpose for which it was created. A hammer nails down. A drill tightens or loosens. A saw cuts. A ladder is utilized to extend one's reach. And it is the job of the contractor to know what tool to use to complete the task at hand.

As you read, it is my hope that I will serve as a coach to help you get to your best life. What is your best life? It is your winning life in Jesus. To accomplish this goal, you need tools. So throughout this book, you will receive numerous tools to renovate your life. You will be equipped with principles that, if applied, have the capacity to radically transform the canvas of your life. I am excited about the journey you are about to embark upon and I am confident you will never be the same. So take a deep breath and let's get ready to *Get God Involved*!

CHAPTER ONE

GET UP

John 5:2-9

"By the Sheep Gate in Jerusalem there is a pool, called Bethesda in Hebrew, which has five colonnades. Within these lay a large number of the sick — blind, lame, and paralyzed — waiting for the moving of the water, because an angel would go down into the pool from time to time and stir up the water. Then the first one who got in after the water was stirred up recovered from whatever ailment he had. One man was there who had been sick for 38 years. When Jesus saw him lying there and knew he had already been there a long time, He said to him, "Do you want to get well?" "Sir," the sick man answered, "I don't have a man to put me into the pool when the water is stirred up, but while I'm coming, someone goes down ahead of me." "Get up," Jesus told him, "pick up your mat and walk!" Instantly the man got well, picked up his mat, and started to walk. Now that day was the Sabbath." (HCSB)

◆ ◆ ◆

We live in a world full of sick, blind, lame and paralyzed people. For many, it is physical. But for others, it is mental, emotional, spiritual or relational. Like the man at the pool of Bethesda, they are all waiting on something to happen. They are sitting on the porch of life, hoping for the moment to come when their life changes forever. Well, if you are reading this book, I declare that your moment has come and your time is now. Healing is available to you today.

In John 5, the man had been in his condition for 38 years. The Bible says Jesus could tell he had been there a long time. How long have you been where you are? Are you beginning to show signs of being stuck? If someone was to caption your situation, would unproductive be an adjective to describe it? If the answer is yes, don't worry or lose hope. I have a word of encouragement for you. No matter how long you have been there, one encounter with Jesus can change everything.

> One encounter with Jesus can change everything.

All we need to do is look at countless examples from Scripture to validate this point. God's resume includes: Joshua at the wall of Jericho, three Hebrew boys in a fiery furnace, a showdown on Mt. Caramel with Elijah and the prophets of Baal, a graveside healing of Lazarus, the awakening of Jairus' daughter, the miraculous healing for a helpless, yet persistent, woman with the issue of blood, and more. In each of these stories, when the power of God was released, everything changed. Famines ended, walls came crashing down, sickness disappeared, and dead people came to life when God got involved!

As you read these lines, I release my faith to connect with yours. As we activate the principles of prayer and agreement, I believe the power of God is being made available to you. I decree things are changing for the better. I release the same "suddenly" Paul and Silas experienced in Acts 16 in your life. Your foundation is being shaken. Doors are opening and bands are being loosed instantly!

Healing and restoration is available to you. The question is: do you want to get well? If you do, all you have to do is take action on God's instruction. Get up! Today is the day to take purpose by the horns and start moving toward your destiny! Healing has been released to you. Receive it in Jesus' name!

REFLECTION QUESTIONS

1. What area of your life are you in need of healing?

2. What's been keeping you from experiencing the wholeness Christ died for?

3. Do you believe one moment in the presence of God can change anything?

4. Are you ready and willing to pick up your bed and walk?

Notes:

CHAPTER
TWO

APPROACH GOD BOLDLY

Hebrews 4:14-16

"So then, since we have a great High Priest who has entered heaven, Jesus the Son of God, let us hold firmly to what we believe. This High Priest of ours understands our weaknesses, for he faced all of the same testing's we do, yet he did not sin. So let us come boldly to the throne of our gracious God. There we will receive his mercy, and we will find grace to help us when we need it most." (NLT)

♦♦♦

Whenever we are challenged, it is reassuring to know the person we are counting on has experience. If you are sick, you don't want to be the physician's first patient. If you are on trial, you don't want to be the lawyer's first case. If you are at a restaurant, you may not want to be their first patron. Recently, I was flying on business into a city where the weather was bad. Winds as high as 60 mph were reported and 3-5 inches of snow was already in the process of falling. Interestingly, as we boarded the flight, everyone had a sense of calm. I believe this was because we were all confident that the pilot was not a rookie, but a trained expert. This was not his first flight. He also had experience flying in difficult conditions.

> Let your need feed your prayers instead of your complaints.

Similarly, as we *Get God Involved*, we must exhibit boldness, confidence and expectancy. We should have complete trust in our pilot (God) to handle what we are facing. He has seen it before and come out on top. So, why do we doubt His capabilities when it comes to our individual lives? Well, let me offer a four-letter word as a response: *life!* Life has a way of pushing people from God. When circumstances arise, people detach when they should in fact draw closer to God. When they should be boarding their flight, they allow fear to keep them on the ground. Our *need* is a reason to get to the throne. Let your need feed your prayers instead of your complaints. Get bold and charge in!

"If you boldly go in, you will boldly come out."

Once you have been in His presence, He equips you to handle anything that comes your way. God already has the answer for everything we will ever encounter. As we boldly approach Him, He lovingly and willingly gives us the solution to our dilemmas. Leave sickness, poverty, brokenness and frustration behind, and search for the remedy. I challenge you today to leave the problem and find God. Then, go back to the situation with what God gave you. This is the recipe for handling life's inevitable challenges.

The Bible says when we boldly go in, we will experience mercy and be the recipient of grace. Mercy and grace are two of God's gifts to the believer to assist them with everyday life. The New Living Translation says, *God gives us help where we need it most.* Where do you need help right now? I encourage you to muster up courage and go to your Father. If you will have the audacity to approach Him, He will release divine assistance for your earthly predicament. This boldness I speak of is not in our own capacity to achieve. This boldness is in our recognition that God's help is what we need. As His children, we can rejoice over the fact that He promised to supply all of our needs according to His riches in glory (Philippians 4:19).

REFLECTION QUESTIONS

1. What keeps you from approaching God boldly?

2. What area(s) do you need help in currently?

3. How will you approach God more frequently and fervently daily?

Notes:

CHAPTER THREE

AGREE WITH GOD

Matthew 6:9-10

"Therefore, you should pray like this: Our Father in heaven, Your name be honored as holy. Your kingdom come. Your will be done on earth as it is in heaven." (HCSB)

♦♦♦

Activating and unleashing your untapped potential sounds exciting, but can be challenging. As you commence your charge to a better life and more meaningful existence, the goal is to discover what heaven is saying. Scripture teaches us that our prayer should be that the kingdom come onto earth, as it already is in heaven. We are not reinventing anything. The work has been finished. We are simply reflecting what's already been done. Think of a mirror. Its purpose is to serve as a reflective surface for the image being projected. Similarly, as Christians, we are the surface upon which God projects His love, grace and forgiveness.

For your life to be successful, you must agree with God. It is not the model for heaven to reflect earth. It is the model for what is done in heaven to be done on earth. Your desire as a disciple of Christ should be to fulfill God's plan and blueprint. Choose to agree with His Word, His thoughts, His promises, and His purpose for you! As you agree with Him, heaven releases the ability, power and resources to succeed to you.

> If you will maintain agreement, you will maintain God's favor.

Agreement in concept sounds simple, but in practice, it can be difficult. The flesh does not want to conform nor give its consent to God's ways. The flesh and spirit are polar opposites of one another. Watch what Paul writes in Romans 8:5-8, *"For those who live according to the flesh think about the things of the flesh, but those who live according to the Spirit, about the things of the Spirit. For the mind-set of the flesh is death, but the mind-set of the Spirit is life and peace. For the mind-set of the flesh is hostile to God because it does not submit itself to God's law, for it is unable to do so. Those who are in the flesh cannot please God."* (HCSB)

The enemy desires that we walk in contradiction to God so that favor and blessings cannot be released to us. Satan wants you to be in a hostile relationship with your Father. His hope is that we would be insubordinate and therefore sacrifice the benefits that come with our divine partnership with Jehovah God. Be gentle as a dove and wise as a serpent! Don't take the bait. Walk in the spirit and you will not fulfill the lust of the flesh.

A few years ago in the NBA, there was a classic example of two people not being able to agree. Russell Westbrook and Kevin Durant were both great talents. They played for a perennial playoff team and championship contender, The Oklahoma City Thunder. Together, these two had been to the NBA finals, scored more points than almost any duo in NBA history, and surpassed countless milestones. Yet, they struggled in key moments to work together. When the rubber met the road, many times, they could not agree on the basketball court. Even though they were talented and gifted, they were never crowned champions because they could not maintain agreement. Could your victory be in jeopardy because you are not agreeing with God? Are you gifted, but known for going AWOL? Today, make the decision to reflect heaven on earth and watch the blessings of God overtake you! If you will maintain agreement, you will maintain God's favor.

REFLECTION QUESTIONS

1. What areas of your life do you and God currently not agree on?

2. In what area(s) would you like to reflect God's image more consistently?

3. Who in your life can you follow and emulate as you align with God's plan?

4. What steps can you take immediately to regain alignment with your Creator?

5. What are some of the benefits you can receive by maintaining agreement with God?

Notes:

CHAPTER FOUR

GET ORGANIZED

Mark 6:35-44

"When it was already late, His disciples approached Him and said, "This place is a wilderness, and it is already late! Send them away, so they can go into the surrounding countryside and villages to buy themselves something to eat." "You give them something to eat," He responded. They said to Him, "Should we go and buy 200 denarii worth of bread and give them something to eat?" And He asked them, "How many loaves do you have? Go look." When they found out, they said, "Five, and two fish." Then He instructed them to have all the people sit down in groups on the green grass.

So they sat down in ranks of hundreds and fifties. Then He took the five loaves and the two fish, and looking up to heaven, He blessed and broke the loaves. He kept giving them to His disciples to set before the people. He also divided the two fish among them all. Everyone ate and was filled. Then they picked up 12 baskets full of pieces of bread and fish. Now those who ate the loaves were 5,000 men."
(HCSB)

❖❖❖

In this Bible story, we are able to uncover a key tool from Jesus. The people are hungry and the disciples do not have enough food for the multitude. But before Jesus releases the supernatural power of God for provision, He gives the disciples an instruction. He says in Mark 6:38, *"Sit the people down in groups."* You may be saying to yourself, "That doesn't seem revolutionary." But hidden beneath the surface of those words is a principle that can alter your entire existence. It is this: Life does not change by chance; it changes based on a plan.

> **Life does not change by chance; it changes based on a plan.**

Therefore, organization is a necessity if change is truly desired! In that verse, Jesus was getting the disciples and people ready for a miracle. He was confident of what He would do, but there was some work *they* needed to do. Today, the same rings true. God already knows the plans He has for you. Those plans are to prosper you, not to harm you. His ultimate aim is to give you hope and a future (Jeremiah 29:11). However, there is work you must do before His supernatural hand is released on your behalf. Organization creates structure, and structure is the foundation for a move of God. Take a moment and quickly reflect on your life. Is it chaotic? Are things in disarray? Remember, miracles don't happen in the midst of chaos.

"Organization not only tells you what to do, it tells you what you should not be doing."

It filters your time, resources and creative energy toward God's work, not just good work. Oh to have back the time that has been wasted on dead-end jobs, hopeless relationships, and dysfunctional habits. Unleashing the power of organization allows you to focus and not be so frivolous as it relates to how you live. This tool helps you redeem your lost time so you can direct it toward more meaningful work! Your career, ministry, finances and health can all be positively impacted by implementing intentional structure. Now is the time for you to organize your life, vision and dreams so God can release His ability to perform the unimaginable.

REFLECTION QUESTIONS

1. How do you determine what is or is not a priority?

2. What system or tools will you use to get and stay organized?

3. What area(s) of your life seem to be the most disorganized?

4. How will creating order in your life benefit you?

5. When will you take the first step to becoming more organized?

Notes:

CHAPTER
FIVE

GET PLUGGED IN

1 Chronicles 29:11-12

"Yours, Lord, is the greatness and the power and the glory and the splendor and the majesty, for everything in the heavens and on earth belongs to You. Yours, Lord, is the kingdom, and You are exalted as head over all. Riches and honor come from You, and You are the ruler of everything. Power and might are in Your hand, and it is in Your hand to make great and to give strength to all." (HCSB)

◆◆◆

To have light, you must have electricity. To have heat, you must have gas. To connect to the worldwide web, you must have an internet connection. Each item is produced or provided because of its source. As a believer, God is our source. He is ruler over everything. As the Scripture says, riches and honor come from Him, and power and might are in His hand. In Psalm 24:1, we learn that the earth is the Lord's, and the fullness thereof, the world, and they that dwell therein. God is a one-stop shop.

Near my home, they recently opened a Kroger Marketplace. This is not your run of the mill grocery store. Here, you do not just shop; you have an experience. The aisles are countless and the options numerous. In one store, you can buy groceries, furniture, electronics, and even get a vanilla latte from Starbucks on your way out. One place has it all. Similarly, when you confess Christ as your Savior and come into relationship with Jehovah, you now have access to "the marketplace"! Everything you need, God has. We must believe this. When we do, it will direct how we approach life.

"When God is truly our source, our actions will reflect a deep sense of inner trust in His ability to perform."

It's so important to concretize in our minds who God is to us. Notice I did not just say who God is, but who He is to *us*. It is our viewpoint of Him that determines what He can do for us. God should not be an option or alternative; He's our only source. When this becomes your mantra, you realize you were not created to be compatible with everything or everyone. Think of your cell phone for a moment. Most individuals who carry a smartphone find themselves loyal to either Android or Apple devices. Interestingly enough, each phone has a specific charger that is recommended for transferring power to the device. What is used to power an Android phone will not be compatible with an iPhone. The ports are different. This is purposeful as the needs of each handset are unique. Likewise, you are fearfully and wonderfully made, and your destiny cannot be supplied by just anyone.

When we try to live life with another source other than Abba Father, we will soon find ourselves powering down. Similar to your phone, in your spiritual life, use only approved accessories. Today is the day to disconnect from anything God has not ordained or authorized to be used for His purpose in your life!

REFLECTION QUESTIONS

1. Is God your source or simply an option?

2. What causes you to lose trust in God?

3. In what area(s) do you struggle the most to fully rely on God?

4. What benefits do you see to total dependence on God?

5. How will you connect with your source on a daily basis?

Notes:

CHAPTER SIX

BREAK THE CYCLE

2 Corinthians 2:11

"I have done this so that we may not be taken advantage of by Satan. For we are not ignorant of his schemes." (HCSB)

◆◆◆

The enemy does not play fair. He breaks the rules and has a "win by any means necessary" mentality. The word schemes in 2 Corinthians 2:11 speaks to the craftiness of our adversary. He has large-scale, systematic plans and arrangements in action to trap and entangle the believer. Many times, if we are not alert, we will find ourselves locked in unproductive cycles. Some of these cycles include sin, stagnation or unconscious insubordination to the will of God.

One of my coaches taught me, "Respect everyone, but

fear no one." With this in mind, you should not fear the enemy. However, do not make the mistake of not respecting him. Satan is so subtle in his approach and devious in his intent. If we neglect to use wisdom, we will be doing what we said we wouldn't for longer than we ever should. This is why the Word teaches us to not be ignorant of Satan's devices, lest he gain the advantage over us. Today, we expose those hidden cycles we have been operating in so Holy Spirit can break their hold. Once free, we can jump back into the supernatural life God planned for us.

"Exposure is the first step to extraction."

My sister Danielle Murphy once told me, "The devil deals in the dark!" Before God can pull you out, you must first acknowledge what you are trapped in. In substance abuse support groups, like Alcoholics Anonymous, one of the first steps to recovery is recognition. Members of the group have to confess their name and verbalize their struggle. It is the acknowledgement of the fight that gives them strength and confidence to overcome the tormenting habit. Destroy the enemy's hidden power today by exposing his hand in your life!

While acknowledging the hidden cycle is good, breaking it is better. As we become transparent before God, He will shine His light through us! The greatest moment of intimacy is when we are totally naked before God. This was how the Father created us to abide with Him in the beginning. In Genesis, God's creation was naked and not ashamed before Him (Genesis 2:25). In this

> **Before God can pull you out, you must first acknowledge what you are trapped in.**

posture, we fully understand and know He loves us just like we are. But, He also loves us too much to let us stay where we are! As we identify those hidden cycles that have caused us to repeat past seasons, let us pray to our omnipotent God for power to break out.

Be encouraged. There is no situation or bondage from which you cannot be delivered. God's dunamis power is available to you, and whom the Son has set free is free indeed (John 8:36). Our prayer should be, "Lord, help us break free of the cycles that have trapped us and rendered us ineffective. Holy Spirit, destroy the cycle itself so we cannot return. Allow us to live uninhibited! In Jesus' name, Amen!

REFLECTION QUESTIONS

1. Are you currently in a secret struggle?

2. What cycle needs to be destroyed for you to fully move forward?

3. Have you established an accountability framework to sustain your freedom?

4. How incredible would life be for you if this cycle was not in operation?

Notes:

CHAPTER SEVEN

FIX YOUR FOCUS

2 Corinthians 2:14

"But thanks be to God, who always puts us on display in Christ and through us spreads the aroma of the knowledge of Him in every place." (HCSB)

◆◆◆

One of my favorite sports movies of all time is *Friday Night Lights*. It is the story of a high school football team from Perriman, Texas. In one of the final scenes of the movie, the coach is getting the team ready for battle against a formidable opponent. The stage is set for his pre-game speech before they rush the field to compete for a championship in the biggest game of the year. As the coach admonishes them of the great challenge ahead, he gives them a famous quote: "Clear eyes, full hearts, can't lose." With passion, he instructed the team to play with focus, leave everything on the field, and have no regrets. And if they did that, there was no way they could lose. Similarly, as your coach, I would like to encourage you to do the same. Live your life with tunnel focus. Rid yourself of all distractions that seek to detour you from God's purpose for your life.

Hebrews 12:1-2 says, *"Therefore, since we also have such a large cloud of witnesses surrounding us, let us lay aside every weight and the sin that so easily ensnares us. Let us run with endurance the race that lies before us, keeping our eyes on Jesus, the source and perfecter of our faith, who for the joy that lay before Him endured a cross and despised the shame and has sat down at the right hand of God's throne."* (HCSB)

We should all take a lesson from our Savior, who kept His focus on the joy of His future and endured the pain of His present. This ability to focus is critical to your success as a child of God.

In the 2016 Olympics, we saw how losing your focus can cost you destiny. In the 200-meter butterfly, South African swimmer Chad Le Clos competed against his arch rival Michael Phelps. During the tightly contested race, instead of keeping his eyes focused on the wall ahead, he began to look at Phelps in the lane next to him. What a critical mistake! While he was focused on his opponent, his opponent was focused on victory. Sadly, not only did Le Clos lose the race, but he didn't even medal for the event! This simple example can serve as a metaphor for us today.

> ***"If we begin to look at what is happening in the lane of another, we just might miss our opportunity to perform in the lane we have been given."***

Next, have passion for what you do. Joseph Campbell wrote, "Passion moves men beyond themselves, beyond their shortcomings and beyond their failures." Passion is the fuel that propels you forward in the midst of adversity and in the face of obstacles. Without passion you will not have the drive to continue, even when success is inevitable. Psalm 44:18 says, *"Our heart has not turned back, and our steps have not deviated from your way."* (HCSB) Today, choose to not turn back. Passionately keep taking steps toward what God has ordained for your life. Finally, if you have passion and live with focus, victory will be the outcome. At The Winners Circle Church, we have a slogan we live by. It is this: You were born to win and created to succeed! Confess that right now. Say it out of your mouth until it resonates in your heart. Through Jesus, you have already been crowned the winner. Live each day that God gives with an edge because you know the fight is already fixed in your favor!

REFLECTION QUESTIONS

1. Have you lost your focus?

2. Is your passion burning strong or fizzling out?

3. What's your current mentality toward life challenges?

4. How can you begin to live with "clear eyes and a full heart"?

5. Like Chad Le Clos, what have you been captivated by that has cost you your promised land?

Notes:

CHAPTER EIGHT

MAKE ADJUSTMENTS

Ecclesiastes 3:1-8

"To every thing there is a season, and a time to every purpose under the heaven: A time to be born, and a time to die; a time to plant, and a time to pluck up that which is planted; A time to kill, and a time to heal; a time to break down, and a time to build up; A time to weep, and a time to laugh; a time to mourn, and a time to dance; A time to cast away stones, and a time to gather stones together; a time to embrace, and a time to refrain from embracing; A time to get, and a time to lose; a time to keep, and a time to cast away; A time to rend, and a time to sew; a time to keep silence, and a time to speak; A time to love, and a time to hate; a time of war, and a time of peace." (KJB)

♦♦♦

Nothing accelerates without shifting gears. For a car to reach higher speeds, it must transition from one gear to another. It is the shifting of gears that increases the capacity of the vehicle to gain a greater rate of momentum. Similarly, in our lives, we must be willing to shift gears. Making adjustments is a necessity if we want to accelerate in our walk with God. There is a higher level. You must be convinced of that fact. There is a deeper dimension. There is a greater place than where you currently are. But it will require you to make strategic adjustments. The transmission is what allows the vehicle to shift gears. As the RPM climbs, it is the ability of the transmission to sense that a greater level is expected. That causes a shift. You have to be able to sense in the spirit when it is time to shift gears. The blessing is, if you shift, you will climb higher.

In Matthew 16:1-3, the disciple Matthew writes, *"Now the Pharisees and Sadducees came up to Jesus, and they asked Him to show them a sign (spectacular miracle) from heaven [attesting His divine authority]. He replied to them, When it is evening you say, It will be fair weather, for the sky is red, And in the morning, It will be stormy today, for the sky is red and has a gloomy and threatening look. You know how to interpret the appearance of the sky, but you cannot interpret the signs of the times."* (AMPC)

In this Scripture, Jesus draws a parallel between accurately predicting the weather and being in tune with the spirit realm. Jesus explains to the religious leaders of that day how they could easily interpret climatic trends, yet they struggled to discern the atmosphere spiritually. Jesus warned them that this void would result in them completely missing the revelation of the Son of God. I believe the Holy Spirit is stirring you at this very moment to sharpen your senses. Your ability to have intuition and properly sense God will be paramount to you shifting properly. If you can't sense, you can't shift!

Matthew 2:7-15 supports this thought. *"Then Herod secretly summoned the wise men and asked them the exact time the star appeared. He sent them to Bethlehem and said, "Go and search carefully for the child. When you find Him, report back to me so that I too can go and worship Him." After hearing the king, they went on their way. And there it was — the star they had seen in the east! It led them until it came and stopped above the place where the child was. When they saw the star, they were overjoyed beyond measure. Entering the house, they saw the child with Mary His mother, and falling to their knees, they worshiped Him.*

Then they opened their treasures and presented Him with gifts: gold, frankincense, and myrrh. And being warned in a dream not to go back to Herod, they returned to their own country by another route. After they were gone, an angel of the Lord suddenly appeared to Joseph in a dream, saying, "Get up! Take the child and His mother, flee to Egypt, and stay there until I tell you. For Herod is about to search for the child to destroy Him." So he got up, took the child and His mother during the night, and escaped to Egypt. He stayed there until Herod's death, so that what was spoken by the Lord through the prophet might be fulfilled: Out of Egypt I called My Son." (HCSB)

What a powerful example of being tapped in to God! Joseph has this amazing moment as the wise men come and worship sweet baby Jesus. I can only imagine the flood of emotions those present felt seeing this supernatural gift lying in the manger. How exhilarating and satisfying this experience must have

> If you can't sense, you can't shift!

been. But right after the celebration concluded, Joseph had a divine visitation. He sensed something. During this encounter, he was urged to make a move since King Herod had evil plans to destroy Jesus. Now the key in this story is *not* the visitation. The key is in verse 14. It reads, *"So Joseph got up..."* Therein lies the key to unlocking your future. Joseph demonstrated not just being able to sense the move of God, but *acting* on what he sensed. He moved on what he heard. Take a moment and think of what the world would be like if Joseph didn't make an adjustment! Christ may have never made it to the cross, and you and I would have never been saved!

"Those who make adjustments excel. Those who shift accelerate. Those who fail to do so stall out."

God desires for you to keep shifting and catching the next wave so that you live life with consistent momentum. Whenever we see life slowing down, we must see what adjustment we failed to make. Dr. R.A. Vernon always says, "Don't make excuses! Make adjustments." This is critical for your year. Don't delay! When you sense it, shift it!

REFLECTION QUESTIONS

1. Where have you stalled out in life?
2. In what area(s) do you sense the need to shift gears and/or make adjustments?
3. What could be currently blocking your ability to sense God and His plan?
4. How will you make a concerted effort to "tap in" or "catch the wave"?

Notes:

CHAPTER NINE

PURSUE THE PROMISE

Proverbs 27:20

"Death and destruction are never satisfied, and neither are human eyes." (NIV)

❖❖❖

In this world, people are bombarded daily to please themselves. Commercials assault our subconscious minds, attempting to influence our behavior. We are being directed to indulge in food, sex and alcohol, and to purchase material objects with the hope of finding pleasure. Sadly, many of us fall for this hook, line and sinker. We appease the temporary cravings of the flesh, only to find ourselves in debt, addicted, overweight and constantly chasing the next good feeling.

This is not God's will for us. The flesh will never be satisfied. It will forever crave more. Today, we must make the shift from pleasing the appetite of the flesh to walking in the spirit. The Bible says in Galatians 5:16, *"Walk in the spirit and you will not fulfill the lust of the flesh."* If we are pre-occupied with pleasing God, we won't have any free time to please our flesh! We must become so disciplined in our walk with God that we aren't available when the flesh calls. The flesh will scream for pleasure, but think before responding. What promise from God will you sacrifice by succumbing to the temptation?

James 1:13-15 gives us the answer: *"No one undergoing a trial should say, "I am being tempted by God." For God is not tempted by evil, and He Himself doesn't tempt anyone. But each person is tempted when he is drawn away and enticed by his own evil desires. Then after desire has conceived, it gives birth to sin, and when sin is fully grown, it gives birth to death."* (HCSB)

"The flesh is not trying to get you to your destination, but detour you to an alternative."

I love this Scripture because it denotes the fact that our own desires draw us away. Once our desires gain our attention, sin is birthed. After we linger in, nurture and feed sin, it grows. It matures. It develops. And this is the stage where death takes place. This is not always a physical death, although it could be. Many times, the death is relational, mental, emotional or even financial. If you give pleasure your focus and continue to feed it, you may find yourself lost and depleted.

Do not let pleasure seduce you away from your promise.

> Don't let go of the permanent promises of HIS will for a temporary thrill!

In John 10:10, Jesus secures his position as the promise keeper. *"The thief comes only to steal, slaughter, and destroy. I've come that they may have life, and have it abundantly."* (ISV) The Word says in 3 John 1:2, *"Beloved, I wish above all things that you may prosper and be in health, even as your soul prospers."* (AKJV)

There is a life full of promises God has prepared for you. You may feel the strong, intense desire of your carnal nature urging you to go in a certain direction. And when your flesh is appeased, it will bring about a rush of excitement and gratification. But, in the moment when sin is performed, what we don't feel is the promise of God leaving. The enemy's attack is so great because of the blessing that is on the way. Don't let go of the permanent promises of His will for a temporary thrill!

In the Word, 2 Peter 1:4 gives us this assurance: *"And because of his glory and excellence, he has given us great and precious promises. These are the promises that enable you to share his divine nature and escape the world's corruption caused by human desires."* (NIV)

Today, break out and escape the world's corruption. Choose the promises of God over pleasure from the flesh. As you do so, watch godly fulfillment and satisfaction spring up in you like a well of fresh water.

REFLECTION QUESTIONS

1. What seems to draw you away from God?

2. Do you find yourself being caught up in the culture of the world?

3. Have you ever made decisions that felt good in the short term, but long-term caused you pain?

4. Which nature are you currently feeding: spiritual or carnal?

5. How can you make immediate adjustments regarding pleasure in your life?

Notes:

CHAPTER TEN

SHOW CONFIDENCE

Psalm 27:13-14

"I had fainted, unless I had believed to see the goodness of the Lord in the land of the living. Wait on the Lord: be of good courage, and he shall strengthen thine heart: wait, I say, on the Lord." (KJB)

◆ ◆ ◆

As a high school football and basketball coach, one of the key mental traits I emphasize is confidence. Confidence is the feeling or belief that one can rely on someone or something. It means to depend on or have a firm trust in. So I teach my athletes to trust themselves and believe they can achieve what they are attempting. After years of coaching athletes and business professionals, I am still amazed to see the results a confident athlete or person can accomplish. Confidence is the characteristic that allows a person to produce in the last seconds of a contest with immense amounts of pressure. It's the distinguishing ability to come through in a crunch. Confidence is the mentality that drives uncommon achievers to embrace and shoulder the load when most would shy away. The viewpoint they have allows them to maintain their inner equilibrium and excel in the biggest moments. Confidence!

Do you have confidence in God? Do you believe Him? Do you place your hope in Him? Do you count on Him in the crucible of life to come through? Simply put, do you trust God? Confidence is built off experience.

"The track record of a person or thing dictates if you can depend on it."

Whenever someone is being considered for an employment opportunity, the hiring manager first looks at his or her resume. The manager examines the past accomplishments and historical performance of the candidate to determine if they are qualified for the responsibilities of the job. Well, if you were to interview God for the position of lordship in your life, what does His resume look like to you? Healing, check. Provider, check. Way-maker, check. Faithful, check. Dependable, check. Takes initiative, check. Willing to sacrifice, check. Exceeds expectations, check. Unconditional love, check. Calvary, checkmate!

In 1 Samuel 17, we see the infamous story of David and Goliath. Goliath was a towering giant who intimidated the armies of Israel into paralysis. They were afraid to fight this formidable opponent, even though the blessing of victory would have been substantial for them and their family. But, then enters David stage right. After seeing the enemy and hearing of the potential promotion for defeating the giant, he begins to speak.

Verses 32 through 37 give an account of David's epic monologue. David said to Saul, *"Don't let anyone be discouraged by him; your servant will go and fight this Philistine!"* But Saul replied, *"You can't go fight this Philistine. You're just a youth, and he's been a warrior since he was young."* David answered Saul: *"Your servant has been tending his father's sheep. Whenever a lion or a bear came and carried off a lamb from the flock, I went after it, struck it down, and rescued the lamb from its mouth. If it reared up against me, I would grab it by its fur, strike it down, and kill it. Your servant has killed lions and bears; this uncircumcised Philistine will be like one of them, for he has defied the armies of the living God."* Then David said,

"The Lord who rescued me from the paw of the lion and the paw of the bear will rescue me from the hand of this Philistine." Saul said to David, *"Go, and may the Lord be with you."* (HCSB)

Notice how David recounts the resume of his heavenly Father. He reflects and reminisces on the moments when Jehovah previously came through for him. For my old-school reader, David took the opportunity to testify of what he experienced when God got involved. Based off those experiences, he had *confidence* that God would prevail again.

> **Use the history of God's ability to predict future victory.**

David used the history of God's ability to predict his future victory. If you read the rest of 1 Samuel 17, you see the giant defeated by an underwhelming David, but an overwhelming God!

Today, take a brief moment and think of all the times God has come through for you. Remember the miracles He worked and the blessings He bestowed upon you. After careful review of God's resume, hire Him! God is fully qualified, based off His track record, to be the master of your life. So, will you place your confidence in Him? Will you offer Him the position as Lord of your life? The choice is in your hands!

REFLECTION QUESTIONS

1. Do you struggle to have confidence in yourself, as well as God?

2. Are you currently squaring off with a giant that has intimidated you? If so, what is it?

3. Can you remember two personal experiences from your past where God demonstrated His power?

4. What voices around you have been contaminating your dream?

5. What step of faith can you take today to show God you have confidence in Him?

Notes:

CHAPTER ELEVEN

BE THE STAGE

Isaiah 6:8

"And I heard the voice of the Lord, saying, whom, shall I send, and who will go for us? Then I said, Here am I; send me!" (ASV)

♦♦♦

I had the privilege of growing up in church. I remember vacation Bible school in the summer and getting to church early on Sunday for Sunday School. I have fond memories of the smell of chicken coming out of the kitchen while praise was going up in the sanctuary. Every now and then, at my childhood church, they broke out singing a song entitled, *Use Me*, written by Ron Kenoly.

As the presence of God would invade the service, they would turn it into a medley and begin to passionately sing a song written by Rev. Milton Brunson, *Available to You.*

These powerful songs speak to the concept of believers making themselves available to God. As Christ followers, it is our duty to surrender our talents and gifts to the mission of our heavenly Father. God is looking for yielded vessels. Yielded vessels are people who have given God permission to work through them. They are individuals who have become available to be an instrument for the master's use.

"Many want to be the performance, but God is actually looking for a stage."

Have you become the stage? Carnegie Hall and Broadway, in and of themselves, are not special. However, the performances that have happened at those locations make them legendary landmarks. They are simply buildings, but once people like Frank Sinatra, Ella Fitzgerald and The Beatles performed in these venues, their status changed! Today, make the decision to become a stage for God and watch the performance He puts on through you.

It is amazing what God can do through someone who doesn't have to get the glory or credit. We live in a world where everyone wants to be recognized and receive accolades. Social media has tapped into our self-gratifying nature with the concept of "likes". Conversely, supernatural things happen when we step aside. We have to become silent and let God speak up. The key for us is to become the reporter, not the story.

As we make ourselves available, without our personal motives interfering, the world will be changed. God is saying to the body of Christ, "If you will let me in, I will bring them out!"

> It is amazing what God can do through someone who doesn't have to have the credit.

If you took driver's education, you are familiar with a yield sign. The purpose of the yield sign is to keep traffic flowing in a safe manner. When you pull up to a yield sign, you give the right away to another vehicle. You allow them to proceed while you wait patiently. Let's yield to God! Stop and allow God to proceed ahead of you. Watch what opens up for you!

REFLECTION QUESTIONS

1. Are you available to God?

2. Does God have full access to perform on the stage of your life?

3. Where are you finding it challenging to yield to God's will?

4. Has pride and self-gratification crept into your heart?

Notes:

CHAPTER
TWELVE

BE THE CHANGE

Deuteronomy 30:19-20

"I call heaven and earth as witnesses against you today that I have set before you life and death, blessing and curse. Choose life so that you and your descendants may live. Love the Lord your God, obey Him, and remain faithful to Him. For He is your life, and He will prolong your life in the land the Lord swore to give to your fathers Abraham, Isaac, and Jacob." (HCSB)

◆◆◆

Recently, I was working out at Lifetime Fitness, my local training facility. As I went to use the restroom, I noticed a soiled paper towel in the urinal. You can only imagine the terrible odor it caused throughout the locker room. After seeing it, my first thought was to notify the staff of the situation so it could be rectified. However, I was led to forego that option and handle it myself. I went to the sink area and grabbed some paper towel. While holding my breath, I proceeded to stick my hand in the urinal to remove the object that was causing the foul stench. After completing this gross and disgusting task, God challenged me to not inform the fitness center staff of what I had done. Holy Spirit spoke to me and said, "This is your gym, so take ownership!"

What a lesson!

Similar to my story regarding my gym's restroom, I want you to take ownership for the conditions of your life. Do not acknowledge the problem, then cease to take action. Do something about it. James 2:17 reminds us that faith without works is dead. Why live with an "odor-filled" life or situation, when God has empowered you to change it?

"Don't look for someone else to stick their hands in the crevices of your life and fix it."

Use what God gave you and take action on the source of the problem. God has equipped you to take charge and change what has caused you to be defeated. Step up and be the change. Let God use you to make the world better for others, without taking the glory or credit.

If you are disappointed and frustrated with the world you see, remember it's a reflection of you. Instead of pointing the finger of blame at your spouse, children, boss, ministry leader, pastor or friend, take a moment and reflect on how their behavior may be a reflection of your influence.

> You don't produce what you desire; you produce what you are.

Before we can fully change the outside, we must change the inside. Bishop Michael Jones always says, "You don't produce what you desire; you produce what you are." Our focus must be centered on *becoming*. Luke 22:32 prompts us to always continue developing as leaders. It reminds us that before we can change others, we must change ourselves. As we become, we gain credibility to help others become.

Pray this prayer with me: *"Lord, change me so the world can be changed by me. Change my will, attitude, appetite, affections and direction. Help me to reflect Christ in my behavior, and allow the world to respond to the Christ in me. In Jesus' name, Amen."*

REFLECTION QUESTIONS

1. What in your life needs to be changed?

2. How can you take an active role in addressing the situation?

3. What area(s) in your life need to be developed for you to become all God intended?

4. Who do you need to connect to or partner with to assist you in changing?

5. What are the benefits of you becoming all God has called you to be?

Notes:

CHAPTER THIRTEEN

BE CONSISTENT

John 8:31-32

"So Jesus said to the Jews who had believed Him, "If you continue in My word, you really are My disciples. You will know the truth, and the truth will set you free." (HCSB)

♦♦♦

God is not looking for occasional commitment, but consistent dedication. It is our discipline that leads to our discipleship. Jesus tells the disciples in John 8:31-32 that the true litmus test of their discipleship is their consistency. One definition of consistency is the steadfast adherence to a set of principles or a defined course. If we want to be followers of Christ, we must continue in His ways. That means we should daily adhere to the standard He has outlined in His Word. Moreover, we should stay the course, regardless of challenges or adversity.

As we embrace consistency, our actions will reflect His character and nature. Replicating the pattern of our heavenly Father is only accomplished by aligning our daily behavior with His prescribed regimen for living.

One time, I was sick with chronic bronchitis and a sinus infection. After going to the doctor, he prescribed an antibiotic, steroid and an inhaler. Yes, I was pretty sick. After filling my prescription, I had to take the antibiotic for 10 days, the inhaler twice each day, and the steroid for five days. This was the regimen I was prescribed to be restored to good health. Trust me, it was not easy to maintain. Life, many times, got so busy and hectic that I would miss a dose, or even an entire day's worth of doses. The problem with my lack of consistency was that it caused my illness to linger longer. I did not remain consistent with the recommended medication plan.

> It is our discipline that leads to our discipleship.

Today, God is challenging you to stay on course by staying in His Word. He has prescribed a winning formula for you. If executed with a maniacal focus, victory is your only option. Please understand, my friend, the Word in and of itself is not enough to make us free. Now, I can hear my super religious readers hitting the floor as they faint after having read that statement. But give me a moment to explain. We know the Word is alive, active and sharper than a two-edged sword (Hebrews 4:12). And, of course, whenever God says something, it is settled.

"But the Word alone, without the action of the individual, produces no results. It is the application of the Word that makes us free."

Hearing and being knowledgeable of God's Word is just the first step. Discipleship happens when we actually execute what the Word says. James 1:22 says don't deceive yourself by hearing and not doing. John 8:31 says if we continue, remain faithful, stick to and live in accordance with God's Word, then we are His disciples. Make the decision to not let go of the Word, but to hold on for dear life. If we will be faithful to the Word, it will be fruitful for us!

REFLECTION QUESTIONS

1. In what area(s) of your life do you struggle to demonstrate consistency?

2. What steps can you take to become more consistent?

3. Who will hold you accountable for your renewed commitment to being disciplined?

4. What are the perceived benefits to you for exhibiting a lifestyle of consistency?

Notes:

CHAPTER
FOURTEEN

STAY IN NEED

1 Samuel 13:1-14

"Saul was 30 years old when he became king, and he reigned 42 years over Israel. He chose 3,000 men from Israel for himself: 2,000 were with Saul at Michmash and in Bethel's hill country, and 1,000 were with Jonathan in Gibeah of Benjamin. He sent the rest of the troops away, each to his own tent.

Jonathan attacked the Philistine garrison that was in Geba, and the Philistines heard about it. So Saul blew the ram's horn throughout the land saying, "Let the Hebrews hear!" And all Israel heard the news, "Saul has attacked the Philistine garrison, and Israel is now repulsive to the Philistines." Then the troops were summoned to join Saul at Gilgal.

The Philistines also gathered to fight against Israel: 3,000 chariots, 6,000 horsemen, and troops as numerous as the sand on the seashore. They went up and camped at Michmash, east of Beth-aven.

The men of Israel saw that they were in trouble because the troops were in a difficult situation. They hid in caves, thickets, among rocks, and in holes and cisterns. Some Hebrews even crossed the Jordan to the land of Gad and Gilead.

Saul, however, was still at Gilgal, and all his troops were gripped with fear. He waited seven days for the appointed time that Samuel had set, but Samuel didn't come to Gilgal, and the troops were deserting him. So Saul said, "Bring me the burnt offering and the fellowship offerings." Then he offered the burnt offering.

Just as he finished offering the burnt offering, Samuel arrived. So Saul went out to greet him, and Samuel asked, "What have you done?"

Saul answered, "When I saw that the troops were deserting me and you didn't come within the appointed days and the Philistines were gathering at Michmash, I thought: The Philistines will now descend on me at Gilgal, and I haven't sought the Lord's favor. So I forced myself to offer the burnt offering.

Samuel said to Saul, "You have been foolish. You have not kept the command which the Lord your God gave you. It was at this time that the Lord would have permanently established your reign over Israel, but now your reign will not endure. The Lord has found a man loyal to Him, and the Lord has appointed him as ruler over His people, because you have not done what the Lord commanded." This story is an incredible example of what can happen when we don't follow God's instructions. But before we condemn Saul, let's take a step back and survey his dilemma. His army is deserting him and has fallen into fear. His enemy has assembled its troops, cavalry and arsenal to launch an attack against him. He is grossly outnumbered." (HCSB)

◆◆◆

If we would be honest, he actually had been patient in regards to the timeline the man of God had set. So my heart goes out to him as I can sense the pressure he was under. But it is out of this place that God desires to teach us a principle. You cannot do *for* God if you don't do *with* God! The moment we stop needing God to do it is the moment God stops working through it. Saul had depended on God his entire reign. And due to this behavior, he saw a display of God's power on his behalf on multiple occasions. But the one time he took matters into his own hands was the time God removed His hand.

Whenever we cease to rely on God to do what we do, we cancel His grace from being made available to us to do it! Think of your life and how God's grace empowers you to succeed as a parent, spouse, employee, entrepreneur, ministry leader or pastor. We must always remember it is Him working through us that allows us to accomplish what we have. If we will produce *for* God, we must rely *on* God.

> **You cannot do for God if you don't do with God!**

We must come to the conclusion that living without Him is not a choice. God is not an option, but a necessity! He is not a luxury, but a non-negotiable.

As believers, it is our responsibility to rely on God's process, even when it does not make sense. God never asked us to understand; He asked us to obey. He never commanded us to figure it all out. He simply requires that we comply. Let us take a lesson from our brother Saul and not take matters into our own hands. Don't do it without God's help, nor operate outside His way. As Peter Scazzero wrote in the

Emotionally Healthy Leader, "Do God's will, his way and in his timing!"

However, if we were to take a dose of truth syrup, we would agree this can be a daunting challenge. Heeding these divine instructions can be hard to do when you lose the support of people, feel God has delayed what He promised, and sense opposition closing in.

"But, God is prepared to use your current predicament to establish your godly reputation."

When you feel the walls closing in, and when you're at the end of your rope, do like the old folks used to say. Tie a knot and hold on! God will show up. Because how dangerous it would be to see God show up once you have already messed up!

REFLECTION QUESTIONS

1. Can God rely on you to follow His instructions?

2. Do you find it tough to remain faithful to the plan when under pressure?

3. What have you personally experienced when you decided to take matters into your own hands?

4. In what area(s) do you need to see God's grace made available to you?

Notes:

CHAPTER FIFTEEN

RESIST THE NOTIFICATION

James 4:7

"Therefore, submit to God. But resist the Devil, and he will flee from you." (HCSB)

♦♦♦

Resist! Fight back! Stand strong against the forces that are trying to overwhelm you. However, you cannot resist until you submit. Submission means to surrender to the will and authority of a superior force. Coming under God is what enables and empowers you to get away from the enemy. The Scripture says to submit to God first, then resist the devil. I think it is essential that we do not ignore the order that is outlined. Submit first, then you will have the resources to take your stand against the devil!

Ephesians 6:10-17 says, *"Finally, be strengthened by the*

Lord and by His vast strength. Put on the full armor of God so that you can stand against the tactics of the Devil. For our battle is not against flesh and blood, but against the rulers, against the authorities, against the world powers of this darkness, against the spiritual forces of evil in the heavens. This is why you must take up the full armor of God, so that you may be able to resist in the evil day. And having prepared everything, take your stand. Stand, therefore, with truth like a belt around your waist, righteousness like armor on your chest, and your feet sandaled with readiness for the gospel of peace. In every situation take the shield of faith, and with it you will be able to extinguish all the flaming arrows of the evil one. Take the helmet of salvation, and the sword of the Spirit, which is God's word."

What amazing protection we have to survive the attacks of our adversary. By equipping ourselves with God's armor, we can *resist and stand*!

"God is the superior force, not the object, emotion, person or situation you are resisting."

We cannot be shocked when the enemy is present if we have not objected his presence. When the devil rears his ugly head, tell him, "NO!" And mean it when you say it. Tell him you are God's child and are submitted to God's will and plan. Will you have temptation come knocking at your door? Yes. Will you feel some type of way at moments and be seduced by your fleshly cravings? Yes. Will you have desires that, at the time, feel so right but, in the grand scheme of things, are so wrong? Most definitely. But, it is then that you have to call on the Holy Spirit resting on the inside of you and resist.

Most of you reading this book have a cell phone. One of the commonly used features on your device is text messaging. This is the concept whereby an individual can send you a written message that is electronically retrieved on your phone for immediate viewing. However, just because you received the message doesn't mean you have to open it. You can choose to ignore the alert. Similarly, when the enemy sends messages your way, don't open them. Choose to protect your spirit against the temptation of sin. Make the

> We can't be shocked when the enemy is present if we have not objected his presence.

decision to no longer be affected by the enemy's presence by resisting his notifications.

If you will resist, he will flee. If you say, "No," the devil has got to go. You are submitted to God and the hosts of heaven are defending your "Yes" to the Father. Pray for submission today. Pray that you will yield to, capitulate, accept, comply with and consent to God's way. God is the superior force, not the object, emotion, person or situation you are resisting. At times, we can feel so powerless against the attacks of the enemy. But when we remember to submit to God, we are equipped with another gear. As God gets involved, we are able to stand in the face of opposition and watch Him work. God is saying, "Bear down. The test is almost over. You are on the verge of breaking through. Don't surrender or quit." Let these words leap off the page and serve as reminder to keep fighting. The tool is in your hands now. Submit, resist and watch the devil flee!

REFLECTION QUESTIONS

1. Do you find it difficult to resist or deny your flesh?

2. Are you currently submitted to God, or do you find yourself rebelling against His will for you?

3. Have you found yourself more open to temptation? If so, why?

4. How can you daily arm yourself to take a righteous stand?

Notes:

CHAPTER SIXTEEN

FORGET THE PAST

Philippians 3:13-14

"Brothers, I do not consider myself to have taken hold of it. But one thing I do: Forgetting what is behind and reaching forward to what is ahead, I pursue as my goal the prize promised by God's heavenly call in Christ Jesus." (HCSB)

♦♦♦

You cannot lay hold of it if you won't forget about that. What is the "it"? The "it" is your future, fulfilled potential and the manifestation of God's best for your life. The "that" is the hurt, pain and disappointment of yesterday. You cannot possess the blessings of your future if you are preoccupied with the burdens of the past. Forget what's behind so you can reach toward what is ahead.

Your efforts always follow your focus. Think of a sprinter. As they race, their eyes are fixed forward toward the finish line. To look back would be a colossal mistake. It would slow them down greatly and hinder their forward momentum. Similarly, make the decision to develop forward focus so your efforts, talents and resources can *push* you toward greatness.

Why is forward focus so important, yet difficult to achieve? It is challenging because the enemy does not allow you to race alone. He is constantly throwing things at you in the lanes of life. And, if not careful, we can easily become distracted and lose concentration. When the enemy brings up a replay of your old behavior, forget about it. If God has forgotten, why must we remember? Don't miss today's miracle because you are fixated on yesterday's misery!

Forget, reach, then press. This is a divine process to victory for the believer. Forget what is in your past. Reach forward with focus to your future. Press beyond all resistance and opposition to lay hold to your God-given promise. Life can be a press. And, if not careful, we can allow the pressure to drive us to surrender. But, be encouraged. The pressure is designed to develop you, not devour you.

> **Don't miss today's miracle because you are fixated on yesterdays misery.**

If you have ever flown on an airplane, you are familiar with the term "cabin pressure". Cabin pressurization is a process in which conditioned air is pumped into the cabin of an aircraft. The purpose is to create a safe and comfortable environment for passengers and crew flying at high altitudes. Because God has designed for you to live at such a high level, there is a need for pressure. The pressure is an indication of where you are headed! You are traveling up, so God has to give you pressure where you are now. As author Mark Divine wrote in *The Way of a Seal*, "Embrace the suck." If you can handle the tough, arduous predicaments of life, I declare things are about to take off!

"*Forget what is in your past. Reach forward with focus to your future. And press beyond all feelings, resistance and opposition to lay hold to your God-given promise.*"

REFLECTION QUESTIONS

1. In what area(s) of your life do you feel stuck?
2. How has your past affected your present thinking and decision making?
3. Why is it so difficult to forgive ourselves of past mistakes?
4. What goal do you currently feel led to press toward?

Notes:

CHAPTER SEVENTEEN

DEVELOP NEW HABITS

Matthew 12:43-45

"When an unclean spirit comes out of a man, it roams through waterless places looking for rest but doesn't find any. Then it says, 'I'll go back to my house that I came from.' And returning, it finds the house vacant, swept, and put in order. Then off it goes and brings with it seven other spirits more evil than itself, and they enter and settle down there. As a result, that man's last condition is worse than the first. That's how it will also be with this evil generation."
(HCSB)

❖❖❖

Many say the best way to break an old habit is to replace it with a new one. What habits are you currently living with that you desire to be rid of? I would like to suggest identifying a preferred habit and beginning to execute it. That's how you break old habits. Light and darkness don't co-exist. One cancels the other. When light appears, darkness is dispelled. In 1 John 1:5, we find out that God is light, and in Him there is no darkness at all. When you shine the light on that dark habit, its hold must break! Recently, I went to grab a coat out of the closet. Upon doing this, I realized the hanger I was utilizing for the garment was broken. However, I continued using it, despite its condition. It was broken, yet I still placed something of value on it. At that moment, God rebuked me and said, "How long will you use broken things?" Instantly, I had to re-evaluate my mindset and adjust my expectation.

God desires that we stop using broken things. In 2 Corinthians 5:17, it says, *"Therefore if any man be in Christ, he is a new creation. Old things have passed away and behold all things have become new!"*

Since you are a new person in Christ, move on to new behaviors, tactics and strategies. This change will bring about fresh results and a different outcome. Don't be spiritually born again, yet reflecting the old man in mentality and decision making.

> ***"Light and darkness don't co-exist.***
> ***One cancels the other."***

The definition of replace is to fill the role of. It means to occupy the position previously held by another. The best way to get the devil out is to put God in! As kids, we all played musical chairs. We know there are not enough chairs for each person, so it is imperative to sit down so you are not called "out". As a believer, work to give the devil no place by replacing his thoughts, desires and plans with God's. Sit the Word down in your mind and heart so the enemy has no place. This is why Psalm 119:11 says, *"Your word have I hidden in my heart that I may not sin against you."*

God does no co-habitate. He is jealous and possessive of His children. Deuteronomy 4:23-24 says, *"Be careful not to forget the covenant of the Lord your God that He made with you, and make an idol for yourselves in the shape of anything He has forbidden you. For the Lord your God is a consuming fire, a jealous God."*

> **The best way to get the devil out is to put God in.**

God does not share space. He wants 100%. Matthew 22:35-38 says, *"Teacher, which command in the law is the greatest?" He said to him, "Love the Lord your God with all your heart, with all your soul, and with all your mind. This is the greatest and most important command."*

Simply put, He wants it all. When you have sacrificed what He has, you could understand why. God gave His Son for us, so His demand is that we give all for Him. Although the sacrifice may be demanding, have confidence that the fruit from your seed will pay eternal dividends!

REFLECTION QUESTIONS

1. What unproductive habit(s) do you need to break?

2. What in your life is broken, yet you refuse to make adjustments?

3. How are you currently giving your all to God?

4. What information do you need to support your new life in Christ?

Notes:

CHAPTER EIGHTEEN

TURN ON THE LIGHT

1 John 1:5-9

"Now this is the message we have heard from Him and declare to you: God is light, and there is absolutely no darkness in Him. If we say, "We have fellowship with Him," yet we walk in darkness, we are lying and are not practicing the truth. But if we walk in the light as He Himself is in the light, we have fellowship with one another, and the blood of Jesus His Son cleanses us from all sin. If we say, "We have no sin," we are deceiving ourselves, and the truth is not in us. If we confess our sins, He is faithful and righteous to forgive us our sins and to cleanse us from all unrighteousness." (HCSB)

◆◆◆

Almost 20 years ago, I was in a service at New Mt. Moriah and Bishop Michael Jones ministered a sermon entitled, "Could it be that you are living a lie?" That word, even decades later, still rings loud in my spirit. The man of God passionately declared that it is possible to be in church, yet waste our time living lies. The New Living Translation of 1

John 1:5-9 tells us we are lying when we say we have fellowship with God, yet go on living in spiritual darkness. What a powerful statement as 83% of Americans claim to be Christian in a recent poll conducted by Encyclopedia Brittannica. But, if we are holding ourselves to the standard of the Scripture, we may not be telling the truth. In the words of a pastor friend of mine, we need to stop all that lying!

It's time to walk in truth and turn the light of Christ on. It's time to stop deceiving ourselves by thinking we have a relationship with God that our lifestyles and behavior do not support. How can we be in relationship with God, yet mistreat our neighbor? How can we claim we are His children, yet display anger and bitterness, and operate in unforgiveness? How can we assert that we are citizens in His Kingdom, but be so insensitive and insubordinate to the instructions of our King? God does not operate in darkness. He displaces it. If we are experiencing a dark area, turn the light of God on and the darkness must be dispelled.

> ***"The closer you walk with God, the less darkness you will live in. The more your life aligns with God's Word, the more successful you will be."***

As you read these lines, take comfort in knowing my intent is not to condemn. God forbid! My motive is to compassionately confront so that you can enjoy the fruit of an authentic relationship with God. Whatever you have done and wherever you are, the blood of Jesus is available to cleanse you from all sin. There is no sin so horrid or detestable that the blood cannot wash you clean from it. Maybe it's adultery, fornication, addiction, robbery, gossiping, murder or jealousy. But nothing can stand against that fountain filled with blood, flowing from the Savior's veins. It is there, as a sinner, we can plunge and lose all our guilt and stain.

Although the blood carries life-changing power, it cannot reach us until we turn the light on. In 1 John 1:7, it says, *"Walk in the light, as he is in the light, and we will have fellowship with one another, and the blood of Jesus his Son cleanses us from all sin."* Change takes place when we walk in the light. Take a moment and consider how it feels to come into your home at night. Because the house is dark, you cannot see clearly. In this environment, you have to feel your way around so that you do not run into anything. But, the moment you find the light switch, everything changes. Similarly, as we find God, who is our light switch, and turn on our relationship with Him, everything shifts. Trust me, beloved. Whenever God gets involved, you can expect results. I am a living witness that the blood of our crucified Savior covers and takes away sin. I serve as proof that the blood still works. The enemy can't keep you separated from the Father.

There is power in the blood. Today, we must choose to leave darkness. Now is the time for you to align your lifestyle with His Word. The closer you walk with God, the less darkness you will live in. The more your life aligns with God's Word, the more successful you will be.

REFLECTION QUESTIONS

1. Are you currently walking in the light?

2. How do you prevent yourself from living a lie?

3. Have you meditated on the power of the blood of Jesus lately?

4. What experience do you need to be cleansed from?

Notes:

CHAPTER
NINETEEN

EXPRESS YOUR GRATITUDE

Psalm 136:1-4

"Give thanks to the Lord, for He is good. His love is eternal. Give thanks to the God of gods. His love is eternal. Give thanks to the Lord of lords. His love is eternal. He alone does great wonders. His love is eternal." (HCSB)

◆◆◆

Recently, I was traveling for business in Pittsburgh, Pennsylvania and needed car service to make it to an appointment. The driver was a gentleman in his mid 50's. While riding with him, I learned he had been downsized from his position in pharmaceutical sales after many years of faithful service. As he drove me to my meeting, he mentioned having received multiple offers for other positions since his layoff. However, the issue was the amount he was projected to make was less than what he was paid 20 years ago! Due to these circumstances, he decided to drive for Uber to take care of his expenses.

As I sat in that man's vehicle, one word hit me like a freight train: gratitude! God reminded me that I work in the same profession as that gentleman and have been through multiple downsizings. Six of them, in fact. Yet, through them all, I am still here and employed. Only God! Sometimes we have to take a moment and reflect on what God has really done for us. We have to step away from bills, jobs, to-do lists and the pressures of life, and remember how good God has been.

In the back of that car, I had to silently praise God as I realized how blessed I was. A few Scriptures took on entirely new meanings as I remembered the faithfulness of God. Psalm 34:1-3 says, *"I will bless the Lord at all times: his praise shall continually be in my mouth. My soul shall make her boast in the Lord: the humble shall hear thereof, and be glad. O magnify the Lord with me, and let us exalt his name together."*

Psalm 150:1-6 says, *"Hallelujah! Praise God in His sanctuary. Praise Him in His mighty heavens. Praise Him for His powerful acts; praise Him for His abundant greatness. Praise Him with trumpet blast; praise Him with harp and lyre. Praise Him with tambourine and dance; praise Him with flute and strings. Praise Him with resounding cymbals; praise Him with clashing cymbals. Let everything that breathes praise the Lord. Hallelujah!"*

I realized that since I had breath in my body, praise was not just an option; it was my duty. It was not a suggestion, but a mandate. When we truly recognize how incredible God's demonstration of love has been toward us, to respond to Him with passionate worship only makes sense. When you acknowledge the wonders He has performed, adoration is what you give Him. Be grateful today. Appreciate the favor of God in and on your life. Never take it for granted. Let your attitude be one of gratitude!

REFLECTION QUESTIONS

1. Do you have an attitude of gratitude or entitlement?

2. How do you exhibit thankfulness on a daily basis?

3. What are you currently grateful for?

4. How can you become more aware and mindful of God's goodness toward you?

Notes:

CHAPTER TWENTY

OPERATE IN OBEDIENCE

1 Samuel 15:22

"But Samuel replied, "What is more pleasing to the LORD: your burnt offerings and sacrifices or your obedience to his voice? Listen! Obedience is better than sacrifice, and submission is better than offering the fat of rams." (NLV)

◆◆◆

Recently, I went to a local TGI Friday's restaurant to pick up a carry out. Normally, I go to the location by my home. But this night, I felt led to go to a different site. As I journeyed to the restaurant, I called ahead to place my order. Immediately, I was irritated at the lack of professionalism and customer service by the receptionist. I was on hold multiple times and, unbeknownst to me, she stopped taking my order and went to seat customers. It was at this point that anger began to rise inside of me like Niagara Falls. So, to escalate my issue, I asked to speak to the person in charge. The manager got on the phone and, sadly, my experience with her was not much better.

Nonetheless, I kept pushing through and finally got my order placed. Once I got to the restaurant, I bust out laughing at how horribly the establishment was run. It was like a food circus. As I patiently waited to be served, I asked God, "Why did you have me come here?" I did not hear any response. Once I got home and began to organize the food I ordered, I found an extra box of mozzarella cheese sticks in the bag. As I opened the bag and saw them, I giggled. You have to know my love for food to truly understand the level of joy that overtook me.

It was then that God said to me, "Don't ever doubt where I send you. Whenever I am involved, there is a blessing in motion you can't see!" Sometimes when we follow God's directions, it can seemingly, on the surface, go from bad to worse. But even when it looks bad, God is working it out for your good. That's why Romans 8:28 says, *"We know that all things work together for the good of those who love God: those who are called according to His purpose."*

God has a master plan in place and His strategy is

perfect. It is our responsibility to stay faithful to His process. If we will be obedient, we will be recipients of the blessing. As Christ followers, we have to be determined to stay disciplined in our compliance to God's instructions.

"Don't miss the promise of the location because of the current frustration."

God said, "Go," but He didn't say it would be easy. But if we obey, in due time, He will uncover a blessing we had not even planned for, nor have room for. If you reflect back on my restaurant example, I had not ordered the extra box of cheese sticks. In fact, I didn't even have enough stomach capacity to eat them all. But regardless of what I ordered and had space for, it was in my possession. In the same way, when you are obedient to God, He will relinquish blessings you didn't request and promises you don't have enough room to contain. The key to a successful life is in our ability to follow God's instructions.

> There is a blessing in motion you can't see.

Deuteronomy 28:1-13 solidifies this: *"Now if you faithfully obey the Lord your God and are careful to follow all His commands I am giving you today, the Lord your God will put you far above all the nations of the earth. All these blessings will come and overtake you, because you obey the Lord your God: You will be blessed in the city and blessed in the country. Your descendants will be blessed, and your land's produce, and the offspring of your livestock, including the young of your herds and the newborn of your flocks. Your basket and kneading bowl will be blessed. You will be blessed when you come in and blessed when you go out. The Lord will cause the enemies who rise up against you to be defeated before you. They will march out against you from one direction but flee from you in seven directions. The Lord will grant you a blessing on your storehouses and on everything you do; He will bless you in the land the Lord your God is giving you. The Lord will establish you as His holy people, as He swore to you, if you obey the commands of the Lord your God and walk in His ways. Then all the peoples of the earth will see that you are called by Yahweh's name, and they will stand in awe of you.*

The Lord will make you prosper abundantly with children, the offspring of your livestock, and your land's produce in the land the Lord swore to your fathers to give you. The Lord will open for you His abundant storehouse, the sky, to give your land rain in its season and to bless all the work of your hands. You will lend to many nations, but you will not borrow. The Lord will make you the head and not the tail; you will only move upward and never downward if you listen to the Lord your God's commands I am giving you today and are careful to follow them." (HCSB)

REFLECTION QUESTIONS

1. What blessing have you forfeited due to disobedience?

2. How can you make obedience a priority in your relationship with God?

3. What steps do you need to take immediately to change your response to God's instructions?

4. What are some of the benefits to living a life of obedience?

Notes:

CHAPTER
TWENTY-ONE

BE PATIENT

Psalm 27:14

"Wait on the Lord: be of good courage, and he shall strengthen thine heart: wait, I say, on the Lord." (KJB)

◆◆◆

Miracles are real and they do happen. On a daily basis, we see the supernatural hand of God at work if we will simply be observant. The beauty of the stars at night, the powerful sound of waves crashing on the shore, or the majesty of a mountain towering in the distance serve as reminders of God's ability. If you are struggling to validate God's miraculous power, simply look at what He has done for you! That being said, somewhere along the way, we have been lured into thinking that every time God moves, it will be suddenly. We look for the immediate result and lose track of the gradual progress that is taking place. Just because there hasn't been a sudden change doesn't mean God has not responded. We can see this principle in Daniel 10:11-13. This is a critical component to walking by faith. For many, when we don't see instant results, we downgrade our request, doubt our Creator and lose faith in our pursuit. This mindset needs to be challenged. The miracle is yours, but that does not negate the process.

To every promise there is a defined process. By process, I mean a series of steps along a period of time that must be completed. Once that takes place, the promise is released. In football, it is said you do not have a catch until you complete the process. So you could have the ball in your hands, but if you don't finish the process, you sacrifice the forward advancement. What promises have we sacrificed because we dropped the ball during the process? What points on the scoreboard of life have been taken away due to us not completing the necessary steps in the predefined time period?

Completing the process requires patience. That's why the Word says to wait on the Lord and be of good courage, and He will strengthen your heart. It takes strength to wait. It takes stamina to stand when everything around you says to quit. It takes fortitude not to surrender to circumstance or situations, but to remain persuaded that God will deliver what He promised. Your life has great potential, but you must be patient enough to not settle for good. James Collins wrote an incredible book called *Good to Great*. In it, he enlightens us to the fact that greatness is in us, but so few achieve it. He wrote, "Good is the enemy of great. And that is one of the key reasons why we have so little that becomes great. We don't have great schools, principally because we have good schools. We don't have great government, principally because we have good government. Few people attain great lives, in large part because it is just so easy to settle for a good life."

Today, God is pushing you through the pages of *Getting God Involved* to not be complacent. Hold out for greatness, my friend. Great families. Great marriages. Great children. Great business. Great churches. Great communities! Wait on the Lord and finish the process He has prescribed for your life. When you do, you will realize the magnitude of Christ's capabilities in you. Receive the strength of God at this very moment to wait. And while you wait, work the process and watch the promise show up!

> To every promise, there is a defined process.

REFLECTION QUESTIONS

1. Why is it so difficult to wait on God?

2. What promises has impatience cost you?

3. Where in your life do you desire to move from good to great?

4. Where have you settled, when you knew more was possible?

5. How can you submit to God's process for you today?

Notes:

CONCLUSION

As a coach, your assignment is to prepare your team to compete. Your goal is to make sure they are fully equipped to handle whatever is thrown at them and still come out victorious. Through this journey of *Getting God Involved*, you have been exposed to numerous Scriptural principles that have the power to alter your life's path. In your hands, are the instruments to build the life God predestined for you. In your possession, are the tools to activate and unleash your untapped potential. But, just like a game, the whistle has to blow for you to actually go do it.

You cannot stay in the practice facility forever. You cannot stay on the bench, discussing strategy and methodology always. Eventually, you have to roll up your sleeves and go execute what you were coached on. Let's review the game plan:

- Get Up
- Approach God Boldly

- Agree with God
- Get Organized
- Get Plugged In
- Break the Cycle
- Fix Your Focus
- Make the Adjustments
- Pursue the Promise
- Show Confidence
- Be the Stage
- Be the Change
- Be Consistent
- Stay in Need
- Resist the Notification
- Forget the Past
- Develop New Habits
- Turn on the Light
- Express Your Gratitude
- Operate in Obedience
- Be Patient

The toolbox is set. The plan is clear. The supernatural awaits and your dreams are within reach. Believe what Paul wrote in Ephesians 3:20, "*Now to Him who is able to do above and beyond all that you ask or think according to the power that works in you.*" (HCSB)

Now take action and commit to *Getting God Involved!*

Made in the USA
Columbia, SC
29 July 2023